The Story of Life

HOW WE ARE COCREATING
A TAPESTRY OF TIMELESS TRUTH

DAWN RICHERSON

© 2020, Dawn Richerson
All Rights Reserved

The Story of Life
HOW WE ARE COCREATING A TAPESTRY OF TIMELESS TRUTH

ISBN 978-1-942969-89-1 Hardcover
ISBN 978-1-942969-88-4 Paperback
ISBN 978-1-942969-86-0 E-Book

This book may not be reproduced in whole or in part, without written permission from the author, except by a reviewer who may quote brief passages. Nor may any part of this book be reproduced, stored in a retrieval system, or transmitted in any form or by any means electronic, mechanical, photocopying, recording, scanning or otherwise.

www.DawnRicherson.com
www.Soul-Simple.com

The Story of Life
is your story and my story.

It is our story.

May this story of humanity
connect you to your essential story of life
and to the light, the life, and the love
that is your essence.

Contents

We Were Born of One Light But Rejected Radiance
We Fell into Forgetfulness and Lost Our Way in Time
We Lost Ourselves in a Story of Separation
We Created a Reality Based on False Foundations
We Felt Wounded to the Core and Withdrew
We Retreated to the Places Where We Felt Safe
We Were Dancing in the Dark
We Dreamed a Dream But Lost Our Way
We Succumbed to the Sound and the Fury
We Chose Small Movements of an Infinite Grace
We Saw a River Flowing Home Yet Began to Doubt
We Became So Cynical
We Got Distracted and Missed the Moment
We Became Preoccupied and Saw Life as Serious
We Sent Out an Endless and Ever-Echoing SOS
We Missed What Was Hidden in Plain Sight
We Were Discombobulated by Direction
We Were Bound by Time, Thinking Life Passed Us By
We Faced What We Thought the Final Curtain Call
We Were a Heartbeat from Remembering
We Saw the Reason Reason Kept Us From

We Felt Divided and Still We Were Met With Grace
We Saw the Limitation of Definition
We Were Buried Beneath All the Labels
We Were Held Through What Was Swept Away
We Were Always Searching for Our Home
We Saw Ourselves as Compromised
We Stood on the Edge of Awakening
We Doubted Who We Were
We Longed to Belong
We Were Scared Stiff
We Found Ourselves Flying Blind
We Held Our Breath
We Were Caught Up in Collusion
We Wandered in the Deserts of Our Hearts
We Filled the Days with Noise
We Faced the Terror of Our Night
We Were Bound
We Were Found in Ordinary Time
We Were on a Never-Ending Quest
We Filled Life with the Echo of Endless Questioning
We Lost Our Voice
We Met Life with Resistance
We Chose Duty and Obligation

We Believed We Were Too Late
We Felt Forgotten
We Sacrificed Ourselves and Our Freedom
We Lost Sight of Freedom's Flame
We Sat, Stuck in Our Seats
We Were Entrenched in Inflexibility
We Tried, Tried, Tried and Turned, Turned, Turned
We Were Jolted and Jostled
We Went Full Throttle and Took the Turn Too Fast
We Pressed On and Missed the Moments
We Were Blocked at Every Turn
We Found Ourselves Dismayed and Disenchanted
We Were Oblivious, Chained to the Ordinary
We Sought to Rise Above
We Acted Out of an Inescapable Ache
We Lived Alone in a Story of Separation
We Sought to Salvage Certainty
We Pushed Away the Present
We Chose Cynicism and Contempt
We Chose Denial of the Human Condition
We Were Lost in a Story of Supposition
We Found Ourselves Shrinking in Shame
We Conformed and Compared

We Saw What Was Lost in the Name of Progress
We Stood Apart and Judged
We Fought the Flow
We Stood on a Far Shore
We Were Searching for the Answer
We Were Cycling Through
We Seemed Strangers to Ourselves
We Were in a Hurry or Stuck in the Waiting Game
We Held Our Breath
We Veiled Ourselves in a Perpetual State of Delay
We Saw What Was Forfeited
We Pressed Hold
We Left So Many Dreams Behind
We Were in a Field of Fixed Circumference
We Lost Our Balance in Busyness
We Feared Changing Form
We Were Looking for Life in All the Wrong Places
We Played a Game of Forfeiture
We Were Stalling
We Were Afraid to Trust Again
We Debated Daring
We Were Perplexed
We Feared the End

THIS GIFT I BRING • Dreams for a New World / Spirited Life • DAWN RICHERSON

The Story of Life

GENESIS • **The Inception of Possibility & a Dangerous Truth**

This movement tells the story of **Who We Once Were** and how we are *Awakening the World Within* for a whole new way forward together.

SOMETHING TO SAY • All She Could Not Say / Spirited Life • DAWN RICHERSON

The Story of Life
ACT I It Is the Dawning of Our Lives

BLACKBIRD HAS SPOKEN. There is something we must say. Morning breaks, and we are broken open. It is the dawning of our lives. **WE RISE TO GREET THE NEW DAY.** Things are **coming clear**. We are emerging into a new awareness of who we are. We are waking up. We see now where **we left our wholeness behind**, where we believed a lie about our true identity.

The invitation of this movement is to embrace a **WHOLE NEW WAY OF SEEING OURSELVES.** You reconnect, slowly at first, to **your essential self**. You open to radiant expansion and exponential growth by connecting to your core. **This is the work of formation.** You discover that you *are* light and a unique representation of the **One Light**.

WE ARE LIGHT. Together, we come present to **anchor in this light**. We see ourselves, each other, and the world around us with new eyes. We dare to make **Our Great Return**, coming back to life with a full appreciation of this story we have lived. Willing now live into a new story, we begin by **awakening the world within**. We come to LIFE and live in full expression. **WE BEGIN AGAIN.**

The Story of Life — ACT I

1

We Were Born of One Light But Rejected Radiance

We begin with LIGHT. *Once upon a time:* Light. *In the Beginning:* Light. We were born of ONE LIGHT, radiant and resplendent. All was held in grace. Still, we could not bear the truth of our RADIANCE. And so we cloaked ourselves, hiding from the light we are, rejecting the radiant light of an eternal truth.

> WE BEGIN AND WE BEGIN AGAIN.
> **WE BEGIN WITH LIGHT.**
> WE ARE LIGHT.

2

We Fell into Forgetfulness and Lost Our Way in Time

Such sweeping magnificence was ours. We came so close to TOUCHING GLORY. But despite the cultural and technological wonders we created, we lost our way and fell in time into a deep slumber. Roaming around in a self-created darkness, we forgot we were ETERNAL LIGHTS, carriers of sacred seeds of essence that held the promise of a new world.

> WE BEGIN AND WE BEGIN AGAIN.
> **WE SEEK ILLUMINATION WITHIN.**
> WE ARE LIGHT.

The Story of Life ACT I

3

We Lost Ourselves in a Story of Separation

The accomplishments of humanity were world-changing, life-changing. Still, it unraveled. Even in our utter undoing, LIFE WAS BEAUTIFUL. Yet, through the ages, we began to feel alone. So alone. Helpless. Unable to fix the broken things, to make peace among the warring factions, to feed the hungry child, we sat huddled in darkness, buckled beneath the weight of it all. We began to see the ONE LIGHT as separate from us and ourselves as undeserving of its warmth.

> WE BEGIN AND WE BEGIN AGAIN.
> **WE MAKE ROOM FOR A NEW STORY.**
> WE ARE LIGHT.

4

We Created a Reality Based on False Foundations

Shivering, we numbed ourselves and believed the lie we told: *There is no light here. I am nothing.* We saw ourselves as undeserving of love and the LIFE MORE ABUNDANT. Succumbing to this illusion, we created a reality based on false foundations. Through the ages, we passed through life in a sort of perpetual spin cycle. We forgot our CHOICE TO CHOOSE. We forgot we were creators of a whole new world. We built a world but forgot that we ourselves were enough. At last we awaken, gathering up silvery threads and golden strands, weaving the world within and without. We begin anew, drawing on LIGHT WITHIN.

> WE BEGIN AND WE BEGIN AGAIN.
> **WE EMBRACE WHOLENESS.**
> WE ARE LIGHT.

5

We Felt Wounded to the Core and Withdrew

We found ourselves pricked by life, wounded to the core. We hurt so much that some of us cursed the very NATURE OF WHO WE ARE. We went less and less to that sacred space within. All the while, we scrambled, feeling more and more disconnected from each other and from ourselves. We longed for reconnection. We have only just begun to understand the truth we left behind: the key to *interconnectivity* is INNER CONNECTIVITY.

>WE BEGIN AND WE BEGIN AGAIN.
>**WE CONNECT TO THE STILL CENTER WITHIN.**
>WE ARE LIGHT.

6

We Retreated to the Places Where We Felt Safe

So many of us caved beneath the pressure of others defining us as someone small. Unable or unwilling to enter the SANCTUARY OF THE SOUL, we splintered ourselves. We tuned out persistent alarms from within, retreating to places where we felt safe. Some buried THE SEED OF SELF that is the soul beneath an endless busyness or addiction. Over time, we silenced our song and lost the tune. Still, somehow, our souls remembered. As we awaken again, we listen to LIFE'S GRACE NOTES and tune our lives to the magnificent melody born from within.

>WE BEGIN AND WE BEGIN AGAIN.
>**WE HEAR THE SONG RISING UP AND REMEMBER.**
>WE ARE LIGHT.

The Story of Life   ACT I

7

We Were Dancing in the Dark

Once upon a time, we were walking in a world. Dancing in the dark, we lost the RHYTHM OF OUR JOY. By the time we knew something was not as it was intended to be, we could no longer find our way. We dismissed the laughter and even the tears that might have led us back. Disconnected from ourselves and from each other, we lost THE MUSIC OF OUR LIVES. Slowly and over time, but sometimes in a crescendo of courage that comes in a moment, we choose to be reconciled one to another and to ALLOW OUR SONG TO RISE FROM WITHIN.

> WE BEGIN AND WE BEGIN AGAIN.
> **WE CHOOSE TO BE PART OF THE UNIVERSAL SYMPHONY.**
> WE ARE LIGHT.

8

We Dreamed a Dream But Lost Our Way

WE DREAMED A DREAM and lost our way, believing all was lost. We forgot all we knew. *Do you see it now?* Close your eyes. Step into it now— that MAGICAL PLACE ROOTED IN YOUR SOUL that you convinced yourself was just a dream. This is what's real: within you are worlds upon worlds, an EVER-EXPANDING UNIVERSE where you can become. Listen for your soul's song, life's lullaby that will sing the world awake.

WE BEGIN AND WE BEGIN AGAIN.
WE TRUST OURSELVES TO KNOW THE TUNE.
WE ARE LIGHT.

9

We Succumbed to the Sound and the Fury

The sound and the fury raged. Afraid of being lost in our own confusion, we became a perfect storm of strangers lost at sea within. Avoiding making friends in our INNER WORLD, felt as strangers amongst ourselves in the day to day. Not seeing that we were already WHOLE, we turned away the parts of ourselves and the people and groups we deemed "other than," further separating ourselves. To our surprise, we find that UNITY IS BORN OF DIVERSITY. We choose to welcome all, dancing the colors back into the light, honoring and appreciating the gifts they bring.

WE BEGIN AND WE BEGIN AGAIN.
WE WELCOME ALL INTO THE GUEST HOUSE.
WE ARE LIGHT.

10

We Chose Small Movements of an Infinite Grace

We are awake now. In wholeness, we take our first breaths. With each beat of our hearts we find our unique FREQUENCY OF LOVE. Through small movements of grace, we begin to feel the dance of life. Something stirs within as we begin to listen for the TONES THAT RING MOST TRUE and tune ourselves to the heartbeat of creation.

WE BEGIN AND WE BEGIN AGAIN.
WE TUNE TO THE VIBRATION OF THE HOLY YES.
WE ARE LIGHT.

11

We Saw a River Flowing Home Yet Began to Doubt

Here on the shores of this new reality, we SEE WITH NEW EYES. We are awakening, if slowly, to the realization that all is not lost. There is a RIVER FLOWING HOME and we see we are already on the way! Yet, as soon as we see it, we doubt our capability and capacity. We lose our grasp, yet fail to see this is what is needed. Only in LETTING GO might we begin to move on and find our forward flow.

> WE BEGIN AND WE BEGIN AGAIN.
> **WE BECOME THE RIVER AND SEE WITH NEW EYES.**
> WE ARE LIGHT.

12

We Became So Cynical

We became so cynical. Stubborn, we pushed away the GOODNESS FLOWING TO US. Resisting life's flow, we wanted to have it our way, to live up to all the expectations we had for ourselves, to change the world to suit the way we thought it all should go. We didn't like the idea of HONORING what or who we saw as a problem and cast so much and so many aside. And so we remained detached, smug even. We lost our connection to the SACRED GIFT OF CHOOSING WISELY.

>WE BEGIN AND WE BEGIN AGAIN.
>**WE CHOOSE TO HONOR CHOICE.**
>WE ARE LIGHT.

13

We Got Distracted and Missed the Moment

How did we get so distracted? So sidetracked and off course? So very busy working for something more and a better life someday, we forgot to look around and see WHAT IS HERE AND NOW. All the distraction took us away from the traction of truth and, more specifically, our soul's truth and radiance, that SOURCE OF POWER WITHIN. Having come full circle, we have now arrived in this present day, so beautiful. Will we dare to look and see all the BEAUTY, WONDER, AND MYSTERY that rises up to meet us on our way?

WE BEGIN AND WE BEGIN AGAIN.
WE DECIDE TO BE HERE, TO BE NOW, TO BE HERE NOW.
WE ARE LIGHT.

The Story of Life   ACT I

14

We Became Preoccupied and Saw Life as Serious

We forgot what it was TO LIVE, TO LOVE, TO LAUGH. We told each other to be serious, to get on about the business we presumed life to be about. In all the preoccupation, we occupied the seat of judgment, all the while losing our DISCERNMENT about what truly mattered most. Do you remember the pure joy of greeting the dawn? Can you hear yourself laughing? RETURNING TO OUR JOY, we laugh our way back to life and love. We lighten up.

    WE BEGIN AND WE BEGIN AGAIN.
    WE GET A SENSE OF HUMOR.
    WE ARE LIGHT.

15

We Sent Out an Endless and Ever-Echoing SOS

We were so busy sending out an SOS that we missed the shining SILVER LINING. Do you remember how clouds dance against the blue sky? We breathe the mystery, dancing back to joy. Beyond the echo, there is the revelation of a mystery. Will you dare to receive this MESSAGE IN A BOTTLE for you and for our world?

> WE BEGIN AND WE BEGIN AGAIN.
> **WE LIVE THE MAGIC AND DANCE WITH MYSTERY.**
> WE ARE LIGHT.

The Story of Life ACT I

16

We Missed What Was Hidden in Plain Sight

We've been stumbling over a TRUTH HIDDEN IN PLAIN SIGHT. Message after message, wave upon wave invited to remember and to rise to a higher harmonic. Listen again. Do you remember love? Can you feel it? You *are* love. LOVE IS WHO YOU ARE. We read this message in a bottle: "*SOS: You Are Loved Beyond Measure.*" It seemed so implausible, so far beyond the realm of the world we had come to know. Yet, we began to reconsider and in time to make this, OUR GREAT RETURN.

> WE BEGIN AND WE BEGIN AGAIN.
> **WE KNOW WE ARE LOVED BEYOND MEASURE.**
> WE ARE LIGHT.

17

We Were Discombobulated by Direction

Our way of seeing limited us. Discombobulated by direction and missing MULTIPLICITY, we played a game of opposites, pitting up against down, left against right. We were thinking we might at any moment veer off into oblivion and miss life. Yet, we existed within an expanding sphere of INFINITE POSSIBILITY, all of it held gently in the container of this single shining moment of now. Life expands to meet us in the present with an astonishing array of CLARITY AND CHOICE.

>   WE BEGIN AND WE BEGIN AGAIN.
>   **WE SEE LIFE AS MULTIDIMENSIONAL REALITY.**
>   WE ARE LIGHT.

18

We Were Bound by Time, Thinking Life Passed Us By

Bound by time, we believed life and time had passed us by. We chose not to believe in what was eternal. We failed to see the TAPESTRY OF TIMELESS TRUTH we were creating in the day. Disillusioned, we felt the fire waning and lost hope. We saw the flicker of forever passing by and felt farther by the minute from the warmth of life. Without warning, LIFE RAISES US again to something more. Changing form, we are unbound from the perspective of limitation, and all becomes possible when we begin at the still point of creation within.

WE BEGIN AND WE BEGIN AGAIN.
WE OPEN TO INFINITE POSSIBILITY.
WE ARE LIGHT.

19

We Faced What We Thought the Final Curtain Call

We saw death as the final curtain and called it finished before we had truly begun to STEP ONTO THE STAGE. We marked time mark, falling in line and marching to the beat of the way we always thought it had to be. Yet, we come at last to find we are not found beneath a marker in the ground nor in the achievement of a milestone or a dream come true. We find ourselves and are found in the infinite evolution of unfolding, a LOVE WITHOUT END.

    WE BEGIN AND WE BEGIN AGAIN.
    WE ARE FOUND IN THE GREAT I AM.
    WE ARE LIGHT.

The Story of Life   ACT I

20

We Were a Heartbeat from Remembering

We felt the loss, the love, and all THE SPACE BETWEEN. We ached at all the loss, the senseless suffering. Then grace unfurled its wings and we saw clearly: we are winged ones, held in a wide embrace. A heartbeat from remembering, we are WHERE LOVE IS TO BE REBORN. Hope is not lost where love is found, and we ourselves are found in the moment of letting go. We learned the distinction between a SURRENDER so sweet and the all-too-familiar sacrifice of self.

    WE BEGIN AND WE BEGIN AGAIN.
    WE SURRENDER TO LOVE.
    WE ARE LIGHT.

21

We Saw the Reason Reason Kept Us From

Certain of our demise, we reasoned it was coming to an end. The evidence that LIFE HELD US, in the beginning and in the end, was right there before us: in tender lilies springing up, in the rains falling down, in LIFE SPRINGING FORTH. Reason kept us from trusting the season of what seemed an unreasonable trust for so long along the way. Slowly, we began to reconsider the reason for our endless reasoning and dare to leave our fortress in favor of COMING BACK TO LIFE.

> WE BEGIN AND WE BEGIN AGAIN.
> **WE OBSERVE LIFE WORKING IN OUR FAVOR.**
> WE ARE LIGHT.

22

We Felt Divided and Still We Were Met With Grace

Squeezed by life, we felt divided into increments of time, boxed in, sliced to pieces. Here, weather or not, we were invited to look again and see THE TRUTH OF WE ARE IS UNDIVIDED. The evidence was right there: there was perfection in each imperfect representation. The unification of what had been divided and neatly kept separate, by our own doing and by powers that once held us in their seductive sway, led us to acknowledge we were free, that there was WHOLENESS IN EVERY FRAGMENT of ourselves and reflected in every fractal of experience. We began to find our freedom in the GRACE OF EVERY MOMENT GIVEN.

WE BEGIN AND WE BEGIN AGAIN.
WE UNBIND OURSELVES AND COME TO THE PRESENT.
WE ARE LIGHT.

23

We Saw the Limitation of Definition

Uneasy, we added too much definition, reducing ourselves to less than all of who we are, CREATORS INFINITE. Stepping out of the illusion, we saw, despite all seeming evidence to the contrary, that ALL IS WELL. We were well and always would be. Before we knew it, it all came clear: we ourselves are complete and ever IN COMPLETION.

WE BEGIN AND WE BEGIN AGAIN.
WE SEE THAT WE ARE WELL.
WE ARE LIGHT.

24

We Were Buried Beneath All the Labels

We labeled ourselves a failure, empty, out of time. We buried ourselves, hearts hollowed out. No mistake can bury you unless YOU CHOOSE. This is what we came to see through trials and tribulations. We redeemed the time by moving through and began to see the field of markers we had made of our mis-takes. We returned to the CLEAN SLATE of the new dawn, the spring that is ever born of winter's cold, and the new day we stood within, which we had until now failed to clearly see. Relieved to not be fixed in relief, we aligned with what it is to BE ALIVE.

WE BEGIN AND WE BEGIN AGAIN.
WE KNOW THAT NO MISTAKE WILL BE OUR GRAVE.
WE ARE LIGHT.

25

We Were Held Through What Was Swept Away

We saw quickly that life could be devastating. It can turn in a second, and all can be swept away. There will be unexpected storms. There is the fire that rages on. Yet, as is written, NOTHING SEPARATES US from the love that is God or from God who is love. We will always be held in that love. What was swept away could not and cannot sweep away this one unbreakable and UNDENIABLE TRUTH OF LIFE. You cannot be shaken from it or the tree of life that is, in truth, who we are.

WE BEGIN AND WE BEGIN AGAIN.
WE SEE WE ARE INSEPARABLE FROM LOVE.
WE ARE LIGHT.

26

We Were Always Searching for Our Home

Hopes dashed, we found ourselves again wanderers, searching for our home—for all we thought we had or for WHERE WE HAD ALWAYS LONGED TO BE. We saw ourselves as small, insignificant, the victim of life's circumstance. When we found the FAITH TO WEAVE AGAIN, the world became a better place. We began to see we were not designed to cling to the safety of obscurity. Home is WHERE WE ARE WEAVING and how we are believing ourselves to be home with one another on this planet spinning in the skies.

WE BEGIN AND WE BEGIN AGAIN.
WE WEAVE A HOME OF BEAUTY.
WE ARE LIGHT.

27

We Saw Ourselves as Compromised

We saw our lives as compromised. We viewed life as less than what it could have been or should have been. Bewildered, we FOUND OUR WAY BACK to the undeniable truth of love in time and rested in the unfathomable GRACE OF SECOND CHANCES. We began to open to the unpredictable nature of life and felt, as if for the first time, the sun shining down and how this is a TENDER MERCY that remains unchanged.

> WE BEGIN AND WE BEGIN AGAIN.
> **WE FEEL THE TENDER MERCIES OF BECOMING.**
> WE ARE LIGHT.

28

We Stood on the Edge of Awakening

Consumed by life and our life of consumption, we wondered, when we first looked away from the screens and the projections everywhere, at the weight of life's striking, sometimes terrifying, BEAUTY. Maybe we had not achieved our measure of success as we once defined it or reached the heights of GLORY we had hoped to attain. We saw the potential in the beauty but failed to enter into it. We stood there, ON THE EDGE OF AWAKENING, until that moment we could no more deny the light we had seen as above and beyond was a creation to which we here WHOLLY BELONGED and saw it, as if for the first time, emanating from within us.

>WE BEGIN AND WE BEGIN AGAIN.
>**WE STAND AMAZED AT LIFE UNFOLDING.**
>WE ARE LIGHT.

29

We Doubted Who We Were

We had not known what was in store for us on this JOURNEY we call life. We carried what we thought we needed but forgot to think of the simple provisions, many of which were provided. We saw THE ROAD AHEAD and were afraid. We doubted if we could do it, unsure if we were enough or had enough. Would we dare to step into A NEW STORY outside our comfort zone? Was it possible we could we set our sights on the way ahead with gratitude and the simple joy of BEING ON THE WAY?

WE BEGIN AND WE BEGIN AGAIN.
WE DARE TO TAKE A SINGLE STEP.
WE ARE LIGHT.

30

We Longed to Belong

We longed for belonging and so split ourselves into smaller and smaller categories of BELONGING. In the reaching for, we thought there was not enough for us. We did not see we have ALL WE HAVE NEEDED. When we began to understand that we belong to an infinite supply, we let it go and LET IT BE. Before long, we felt at home and began in time to live at peace with all things within and without, knowing we belong to one another and to ALL THAT IS and has ever been or will ever be.

WE BEGIN AND WE BEGIN AGAIN.
WE BELONG TO ALL THAT IS.
WE ARE LIGHT.

31

We Were Scared Stiff

Unseen forces tore at our TENDER HEARTS. Love flattened us, leaving us scared stiff of being human. We encountered pain in infinite variety. Some of us were stunned to see ALL THAT WAS POSSIBLE reflected back and magnified in the mirror of another. When this was gone, we had no words and no will to carry on. But somewhere within we knew: love is neither created nor destroyed. Love remains. We saw we had come close to LOVE'S TRUE NATURE in our souls. In the breaking apart we had so long feared, we found a new beginning. We were broken open only to discover reflections of a breathtaking light that flowed from from the very HEART OF WHO WE ARE.

WE BEGIN AND WE BEGIN AGAIN.
WE ALLOW OURSELVES TO BE BROKEN OPEN.
WE ARE LIGHT.

32

We Found Ourselves Flying Blind

Out of fire, we flew blind, feeling all was contaminated, rendered null and void. We forgot that, in the context of time, DAY IS ALWAYS BORN OF NIGHT. We became as stars, shooting through the night, propelled by some mysterious grace. Trusting life, we LET LOVE LEAD THE WAY. Living at the speed of love for this journey we have made, we find in the slow changing of the seasons of our lives a natural progression, a RIVER THAT WILL CARRY US in the direction of all the good we seek.

> WE BEGIN AND WE BEGIN AGAIN.
> **WE LET LOVE BE THE FUEL.**
> WE ARE LIGHT.

33

We Held Our Breath

We held our breath, waiting on pins and needles for the end or for some beginning again, unsure of whether we were HEADED HOME or anywhere at all. Breathing in, breathing out, we were suspended in time and space. This was the home stretch, and yet we were already existing in A PLACE OF MIRACLES. Breathing in and breathing out, we began to release our expectation and see things in a different light, a perspective that shed just enough light for the next right step in faith, the first of our soul's seven wonders.

> WE BEGIN AND WE BEGIN AGAIN.
> **WE BREATHE IN AND ALLOW OURSELVES TO BE ON THE WAY.**
> WE ARE LIGHT.

34

We Were Caught Up in Collusion

Wounded or wounding, and sometimes both, we doubted from time to time our deservedness of the good life. Pulled back again from our retreat right to LIFE'S LEADING EDGE, we saw how we had been caught up in collusion, a conspiracy of silence and confusion. We saw how we had pretended to be mere ships passing in the night. Had we dared to believe, we might have seen we were always ON THE WAY TOGETHER. Perhaps we will choose this new way of seeing soon and see that the very structure of belief can be a barrier to A LIFE OF LIGHTNESS and of love.

WE BEGIN AND WE BEGIN AGAIN.
WE DARE TO BELIEVE IN LIFE.
WE ARE LIGHT.

35

We Wandered in the Deserts of Our Hearts

In the deserts of our heart, we wandered, transfixed by LIFE'S GIFT, unconditional, of another way. We stood between forever and this day, pondering. We made the choice to CHOOSE LIFE and the promise of a whole new way forward. Instead of frantically and feverishly working for the future or dwelling in the pain of the past, we came back to life and met the MIRACLE OF THE MOMENT right where we found ourselves to be. Here we began to heal our hearts and the HEART OF HUMANITY.

    WE BEGIN AND WE BEGIN AGAIN.
    WE CHOOSE THIS DAY.
    WE ARE LIGHT.

36

We Filled the Days with Noise

Still, after coming so far, we filled the days with noise. Weary the fake, the fraudulent, and the famous of the moment, we searched far and wide for SOME TRUTH—a truth we simultaneously sought and sought to avoid. We told ourselves truth had vanished from our world. Listening to THE SOUND OF SILENCE, we hear with new ears the beauty of the music of the morning ringing resonant. The deeper, clearer TONES OF TRANSFORMATION could be heard, faintly at first, and then felt as a standing invitation to enter into silence.

> WE BEGIN AND WE BEGIN AGAIN.
> **WE LISTEN FOR LIFE'S TRUE TONES.**
> WE ARE LIGHT.

37

We Faced the Terror of Our Night

The terror of our soul's dark night and the world's difficult passage into a new era became a HOLY GIFT as we counted the stars springing forth from our hearts. Holding this light loosely and with GRATITUDE moved us at THE SPEED OF LIGHT, which is timeless and a wave of grace, toward the world we'd always wanted. Having taken it all for granted and not quite believing life would grant us clemency, we saw we once were blind and knew now all we could not see then. Do I truly treasure that diamond of A STAR THAT LIGHTS OUR WAY? This is the question we began to ask, one by one by one.

>WE BEGIN AND WE BEGIN AGAIN.
>**WE KNOW WE ARE SAFE IN SPACE AND TIME.**
>WE ARE LIGHT.

38

We Were Bound

Bound to a truth that trapped us or cut us loose, we made A NEW CHOICE to refuse captivity. Binding up our broken hearts, we began at last to see LIFE AS FORGIVING and for giving. So we entered into a cycle of giving and receiving, loosening the reigns of the ropes with which we had bound ourselves in time. We stepped into the throne room within, knowing we are FREE SPIRITS, free to choose a life of sovereignty.

WE BEGIN AND WE BEGIN AGAIN.
WE ARE FREE-SPIRITED IN THIS LIFE THAT IS FORGIVING.
WE ARE LIGHT.

39

We Were Found in Ordinary Time

Born in ordinary time, we celebrate our ORIGIN AND ORIGINALITY. We see we have come bearing sacred seeds of essence, meant to be shared in the soil of now. We are AWAKENING THE WORLD as we awaken to the world within. On the most ordinary of days, in ordinary time, we open our hearts to share EXTRAORDINARY GIFTS of life with a world that responds in kind.

> WE BEGIN AND WE BEGIN AGAIN.
> **WE SHARE FINE GIFTS OF ORIGINAL DESIGN.**
> WE ARE LIGHT.

RISE AND FALL • **The Dream We Dreamed & How We Lost Ourselves**

This movement explores **Who We Thought Ourselves to Be** and how we are *Finding Our Forward Flow* from the fertile crescent of hope.

LOST IN THE DREAM • Dreams for a New World / Spirited Life • DAWN RICHERSON

The Story of Life
ACT II We Find Grace in This Day

WE MAKE A SINGLE CHOICE TO BELIEVE. We are **finding our way**, seeking, searching. Life's current is swift, and the stars remind us we ourselves are eternal being. WE RISE TO GREET THE NEW DAY, flying in formation, birds of a feather. **We find grace in this day.**

The invitation of this movement is to embrace a WHOLE NEW WAY OF BEING OURSELVES. As you reconnect to **your essential journey** and understand there is a river of life running through you, you help us all create a new story of life. **This is the work of reformation.** We open to radiant expansion and exponential growth through integration and flow. You discover that you are life, a unique representation of the **One Life**.

WE ARE LIFE. Together, we begin to **articulate this life we are**. Here, our life and work, our past and future, **our being and becoming flow together.** We live now into a new story, **finding our forward flow** as we come to LIFE and live in full expression. WE BEGIN AGAIN.

The Story of Life   ACT II

40

We Were on a Never-Ending Quest

Thirsty, we wandered through life's desert in a never-ending quest, tripped by THE SANDS OF TIME. Hot days, cold nights, and never enough. We began to question and saw then that, in our quest, so much had slipped away. In the stars, we found reflection which led us to remember and RECEIVE THE DREAM that had been waiting there within. We remembered the dream alive, and this was the beginning of our collective choice to immerse ourselves in only what is TRUE TO LIFE.

>WE BEGIN AND WE BEGIN AGAIN.
>**WE REMEMBER THE DREAM WE DREAMED.**
>WE ARE LIFE.

41

We Filled Life with the Echo of Endless Questioning

The sun so bright, we shielded our eyes. Frightened by THE SPACE OF SILENCE, we encircled ourselves and each other, clamoring for attention and answers to so many questions. Unaccustomed to MYSTERY, in a land flowing with milk and honey, still we saw ourselves as starved. All the same, in time, we stopped reaching. We forgot the source of our silent spring and the RIVERS OF HOPE that flowed forth from within. Then, in a rare moment of silent reflection: a flood of truth. Unmasked, we understood THE FLOW OF AN ETERNAL LIFE.

    WE BEGIN AND WE BEGIN AGAIN.
    WE HEAR ALL THAT COMES TO US IN SILENCE.
    WE ARE LIFE.

The Story of Life   ACT II

42

We Lost Our Voice

WE FOUND OUR HOPE and lost it ever so quickly as life's winds shifted. We saw that we had fallen and felt we could never do enough. We felt we could not find our way to TRUTH AND HOPE against such currents. We stopped our singing, that had seemed only a cacophony of confusion. And then we forgot our power to speak truth, and power had its way. Slowly, we felt a desire for something more and SPOKE THE WORD INTO LIFE. In speaking clear, we returned to all that is true.

    WE BEGIN AND WE BEGIN AGAIN.
    WE RAISE OUR VOICE TO FIND OUR TRUTH.
    WE ARE LIFE.

43

We Met Life with Resistance

We resisted CHANGE, having learned to fear what might come next. We pulled against the tide, clinging to the shores we knew and denying the CURRENT, for experience seemed a cruel master. In the ebb and flow, we learned in time to release and then return to LIFE'S CURRENCY and flowed naturally with the constant of change.

>WE BEGIN AND WE BEGIN AGAIN.
>**WE STAY CURRENT.**
>WE ARE LIFE.

44

We Chose Duty and Obligation

We chose duty and obligation, sweeping love's unpredictability aside. We convinced ourselves we were in control, all the while collecting impurities and debris that covered ALL THAT MATTERED MOST. Seeing we had been hardened by life, yet still unsure, we resisted change. Opening up to the flowering of our life, we began to feel THE HEARTBEAT OF REMEMBERING. To feel the joy of freedom, all the while tending to what must be tended to, was the key. Receptivity gave us everything.

WE BEGIN AND WE BEGIN AGAIN.
WE ALLOW OUR HEARTS TO EXPERIENCE CHANGE.
WE ARE LIFE.

The Story of Life ACT II

45

We Believed We Were Too Late

We thought it was too late TO DREAM, TO DANCE, TO LOVE again. We stood in a glorious field, frozen and feeling hollowed out. If only someone might pour in us A BLESSED BALM. But then, where would we go? What would we do? How could we even move in this hard shell? Stretching to feel the gentle waves at THE SHORE OF EXPERIENCE, we peeked out, only just beginning to understand it is never too late. At last we knew THERE IS NO TOO EARLY OR TOO LATE in the movement of coming to trust that we are connected to an eternal source and an INFINITE SUPPLY.

WE BEGIN AND WE BEGIN AGAIN.
WE KNOW WE HAVE ALL WE NEED.
WE ARE LIFE.

46

We Felt Forgotten

We believed we stood in the field alone, forgotten by life. And so we created perpetual stories of lack and missed LIFE'S ABUNDANT FLOW. Our breathing was labored and shallow, and we took all we had for granted, stuck in a cycle of suffering. We were alive but barely breathing. We slowed our pace to connect again to the DEPTHS OF LOVE WE ARE HELD WITHIN. We dared to roll out the welcome mat. And suddenly it was abundantly clear WE ARE NEVER ALONE.

    WE BEGIN AND WE BEGIN AGAIN.
    WE BREATHE DEEPLY AND WELCOME LIFE'S FLOW.
    WE ARE LIFE.

47

We Sacrificed Ourselves and Our Freedom

The pain became so great for some of us that we propped ourselves up as gods, splitting ONE GLORIOUS REALM OF GRACE into pieces and claiming them as our own, dividing humanity into smaller and smaller fragments, a society to which only a select few belonged. We sacrificed the SACRED FREEDOM that is our birthright on the altar of a shallow success. Seeing this, we chose to course correct and to TREASURE THE GIFT SO FREELY GIVEN.

>WE BEGIN AND WE BEGIN AGAIN.
>**WE HOLD SACRED THE FREEDOM THAT IS OUR BIRTHRIGHT.**
>WE ARE LIFE.

48

We Lost Sight of Freedom's Flame

We lost our way. The eternal FLAME OF FREEDOM seeming to have been extinguished, we grieved at the fragmentation and thought it all too late. We lost sight of ALL THAT WAS GIFTED in lives we saw as ordinary. We saw the trappings of success and felt it was too late for a FREEDOM SONG in hearts weary of this world.

> WE BEGIN AND WE BEGIN AGAIN.
> **WE SEE THE HOLY IN THE ORDINARY.**
> WE ARE LIFE.

49

We Sat, Stuck in Our Seats

Caught up in the drama of our lives or lost within its plot, we BECAME THE OBSERVERS. We felt a sense of hopelessness and despair. Our minds numbed to the predictable soundtrack that never really satisfied. Our hearts hardened by the narrowed loop of our choices, we forgot we could get up from our seats and call the scene. We forgot our ability to CHANGE OUR LIFE'S EXPERIENCE. Getting up and moving on, we set the stage for stepping back onto the stage.

>WE BEGIN AND WE BEGIN AGAIN.
>**WE CHOOSE OUR MIRROR, SET THE SCENE.**
>WE ARE LIFE.

50

We Were Entrenched in Inflexibility

Our minds fixed on a particular WAY OF BEING in this world, we were frozen in place. We wanted it to be different, but felt frozen. It seemed impossible. What was the point? We were too young, too old. And so we fell into a pattern, day after day, failing to FLEX the muscle of our minds. Gaining strength, we wiped the sleep from our eyes, stretched beyond the rigidity of unnecessary regulations and emerged into THE SPARKLING WONDER of this new day.

> WE BEGIN AND WE BEGIN AGAIN.
> **WE FLEX THE MUSCLE OF OUR MINDS.**
> WE ARE LIFE.

51

We Tried, Tried, Tried and Turned, Turned, Turned

THE LIVES WE CREATED for ourselves seemed unbearable. Yet, some of us fell in line, vowing to try harder and do better, to follow every rule. Others cast it all aside and turned their backs on everything. In both cases, we left THE LOVE THAT IS here and now behind, giving up on the gift that is the present. At last we stopped the turning, churning, burning desire for what we though should be or who we thought we should become. And everything, everywhere, all at once seemed to CELEBRATE LIFE and our embrace of it.

WE BEGIN AND WE BEGIN AGAIN.
WE SURRENDER THE QUEST AND RETURN TO LOVE.
WE ARE LIFE.

52

We Were Jolted and Jostled

We felt jolted and jostled by LIFE'S SHIFTS. It felt as if we were getting nowhere. Our perspective lost, we failed to see the growth within. We gave our attention over to what seemed an erratic sequence of endless point and counterpoint. Relaxing enough to simply WALK IN THE WAY OF LIFE, we opened up to the joy of being on the way. Awake and aware, we embraced THE ART OF BEING AND BECOMING within the wholeness and without a fixation on fixing.

> WE BEGIN AND WE BEGIN AGAIN.
> **WE OPEN TO FULL AWARENESS.**
> WE ARE LIFE.

The Story of Life ACT II

53

We Went Full Throttle and Took the Turn Too Fast

Life's road was sloping into a new vistas and a landscape of learning, and at last we were LOOKING FORWARD. Again, we took control and sped on to the long-awaited vistas of relief. But we took the curve too fast, forgetting we had ALL THE TIME WE NEED. Taking it easy, we began to find peace in the present. In presence, we were at peace.

WE BEGIN AND WE BEGIN AGAIN.
WE EASE INTO LIFE'S CURVES.
WE ARE LIFE.

The Story of Life ACT II

54

We Pressed On and Missed the Moments

Our eyes yet fixed on the golden destination of our choice, we changed lanes and pursued our FORWARD PROGRESS. Often going through the motions in a perpetual state of half-awake and in a hurry to arrive, we missed so much. Who had time for conversation? Thinking we had no time to spare, we missed the magical moments and all the wonder years. We never thought to simply LOVE THE RIDE and let life surprise us on the way.

WE BEGIN AND WE BEGIN AGAIN.
WE STAY AWAKE FOR THE JOURNEY.
WE ARE LIFE.

The Story of Life   ACT II

55

We Were Blocked at Every Turn

Growling beneath our breath, we pushed the gas and barreled on toward DESIRED DESTINATIONS, wearing ourselves down and wearing ourselves out. Stuck in traffic, we cursed our plight, finding our focus ever fixed on the blocks and failing to find A WAY AROUND. Those blocks became our world, and our way of moving through the world became a game to conquering. In time, we came to see there was another way, TUNING OUR FINE FOCUS to the finer things we had forgotten in our striving through the days.

WE BEGIN AND WE BEGIN AGAIN.
WE FIND A WAY AROUND BLOCKS.
WE ARE LIFE.

56

We Found Ourselves Dismayed and Disenchanted

So much had been corrupted. Where was life's LIFE'S PURITY? No matter how we tried to shed life's dirt and debris, it seemed to cling to us. We sought to cast it off, feeling nothing but disdain. Soon we turned to destruction, spiraling down into dismay and disenchantment with life and with ourselves. We lost sight of the SACRED GIFT, forgetting it was there at all at first. Later, when we saw these miraculous DESIGNS FOR LIFE hiding in plain sight, we nevertheless failed to feel the blessing and give thanks.

WE BEGIN AND WE BEGIN AGAIN.
WE BEGIN WITH GRATITUDE.
WE ARE LIFE.

57

We Were Oblivious, Chained to the Ordinary

Every day, life dragged on, and we were caught up in a drudgery we, through our collusion, created and later came to expect. We tired of our DAILY BREAD, which seemed a meager gift for all our hard work. Around and around we went, oblivious to THE BEAUTY AND THE BLESSING. Sitting down again at life's table, we were amazed by our abundance. Returning to living and giving thanks, we were NOURISHED BY THE GRATITUDE and, though little changed outside ourselves, we moved through life freely and attuned to the fact that we were living in a LAND OF PLENTY.

> WE BEGIN AND WE BEGIN AGAIN.
> **WE GIVE THANKS FOR ALL THAT NOURISHES.**
> WE ARE LIFE.

58

We Sought to Rise Above

Determined to make something of our lives, we sought to rise above the mundane life, not realizing the WONDER OF THE WAY or the beauty of the day. We studied it from afar, all the while closing down our hearts, pretending to be impervious to its SWEEPING GRACE. We counted our coins and made precise notes. We offered pleasantries from a distance, having decided it was the only way. And then one day we saw it differently and tried a different way. We opened our hearts to THE MYSTERY THAT WAS OUR STORY and danced in the light of all that was yet unknown.

WE BEGIN AND WE BEGIN AGAIN.
WE GET IN THE STORY.
WE ARE LIFE.

59

We Acted Out of an Inescapable Ache

One day, we noticed it; the tiny crack that had widened into a chasm between us. Despite our efforts to MOVE THROUGH LIFE unscathed, we fell into its inescapable wound. We could not comprehend how, though we furiously sought to fill up our life with all it seemed to lack, still there was this ache—a hole within our hearts. We focused on faults and forgot to FIND FAVOR, wondering why the ache of empty grew ever larger within. When we thought to slow down and tend to what had fallen through the cracks, we discovered to our dismay LIFE HAD FOUND A WAY.

WE BEGIN AND WE BEGIN AGAIN.
WE FIND FAVOR, NOT FAULT.
WE ARE LIFE.

60

We Lived Alone in a Story of Separation

We decided things. We drew our own conclusions about this life and so focused on our certainty proved our theories true. In the end, we were as alone as ever, having separated ourselves from life and from those with whom we SHARE THE JOURNEY. Operating solo or caught up in competition, we did not see how we were always on the way together. In those rare moments we came together or noticed the PATTERNS OF POTENTIAL made by the waves and designs we made by moving through our days, we began to notice WE WERE CONNECTED despite our insistent belief to the contrary. Tending to what presented, we began to come together in constellations of change and cultivate cooperation.

WE BEGIN AND WE BEGIN AGAIN.
WE CULTIVATE COOPERATION.
WE ARE LIFE.

61

We Sought to Salvage Certainty

There came the startling PRESENT OF THE TRUTH, shaking all our presuppositions about who we were and why we had come. Yet, we were afraid of what SUCH A GREAT LOVE revealed would mean, and so set about reordering worlds, if only to salvage all we thought left to save. Salvaging the salvage operation, we came to comprehend the shocking truth that WE WERE NOT IN NEED OF SAVING. Surprised by such a radiant realization we were changed from the inside out and saved the remains of the day. This was LIFE'S SALVATION. When and where it was accepted, our receiving of life's gift led likewise to the preservation of humanity's trajectory of change.

WE BEGIN AND WE BEGIN AGAIN.
WE SEE TRUTH WHEN IT SURPRISES US.
WE ARE LIFE.

62

We Pushed Away the Present

So it is that LIFE PRESENTED US THE GIFT of the present, and it often came packaged in surprise. We often pushed it away or thought it a trick, waiting for A BETTER DAY. At times, we tore into the gift and then just as quickly cast it aside. We saw the truth that LIFE WAS A GIFT and still persisted in making a case against it, because it has disrupted our plans for perfection or what we presumed that to be. Having sat on the sidelines for so long, we dared at last to say yes to the DANCE OF LIFE.

WE BEGIN AND WE BEGIN AGAIN.
WE TREASURE THE DANCE OF LIFE.
WE ARE LIFE.

63

We Chose Cynicism and Contempt

We demanded our just reward, having sacrificed so much. Having learned to compensate for the LIFE AND LOVE we believed we had to set aside, we fled, fast at first, from the very truth that might have set us free. We settled, bargained, begged, or even stole what we thought should be ours. We met THIS GRACIOUS LIFE with sarcasm, cynicism, and a boiling contempt beneath the placid smiles. We waited for a moment that never seemed to come. Exasperated by the accumulation and calcification that was the result of our contempt, we burnt out and broke down and too tired to maintain our fight for proper compensation, we let go and LET LIFE LEAD US BACK TO LOVE.

WE BEGIN AND WE BEGIN AGAIN.
WE LET GO OF A NEED FOR COMPENSATION.
WE ARE LIFE.

64

We Chose Denial of the Human Condition

We cut ourselves off from the experience of BEING IN HUMAN FORM. We pretended not to notice the body's dialogue, dismissing it outright or treating it with disdain and disregard. Distanced from the body that was blessed, we chose denial of our very FORM AND FUNCTION and so suffered the dire consequence resulting from a choice to interfere with the vessel for our soul's incarnation. We delayed the ADVENT OF AWAKENING from within a body electrified by life and denied the condition of being human. Conditioned to deify or disregard, we took care and began to care about the CONDITION OF LIFE'S VESSEL.

WE BEGIN AND WE BEGIN AGAIN.
WE LISTEN TO OUR BODIES.
WE ARE LIFE.

The Story of Life   ACT II

65

We Were Lost in a Story of Supposition

We felt the stir of a WILD DESIRE. We heard the beating of a different drum. Yet, who were we to dare to be anyone special? We doubted THE TRUTH THAT RISES UP. We wore the labels this world would put upon us all too willingly. We droned on, louder and louder, hoping to drown out all the noise that seemed an endless confusion. We were caught up in the story of who we are meant to be, face to face with the supposed sacrifice required. Facing the CHOICE FOR SOVEREIGNTY, we longed to belong. The longing, before long, led to unity in differentiation ask the key to knowing we belong.

WE BEGIN AND WE BEGIN AGAIN.
WE KNOW WHERE WE BELONG.
WE ARE LIFE.

The Story of Life ACT II

66

We Found Ourselves Shrinking in Shame

Someone somewhere, ONCE UPON A TIME, made a pronouncement and placed upon our lives a mantle of shame. We began to believe we were flawed, forever burdened by the life that was BESTOWED AS GIFT. We tried to set our lives aright, to fit into society. We thought we had been eaten alive, reduced to a shattered offering and so turned away from LOVING THIS LIFE. We felt a shrinking, a sinking, until one day we decided to cast off the mantle of shame and give ourselves the love we had so long and so richly deserved to receive. Rising into a Realm of Radiance, we learned the NOBILITY OF GRACE for ourselves in this time and place.

WE BEGIN AND WE BEGIN AGAIN.
WE LOVE OURSELVES FIRST.
WE ARE LIFE.

67

We Conformed and Compared

We moved through life, just trying to avoid the bumps and bruises, and missed the NEXT OPPORTUNITY WINDOW that is the now. We were constantly looking around, comparing who we were to what we saw. We told ourselves a story about how we measured up—as if life were some competition. Whether we conformed or went against the grain, we ran far and fast from THE FULLNESS OF WHO WE ARE. Catching our breath, we saw the error of our ways and stopped to smell the roses and savor the beauty of the day. Noticing our hurry, witnessing our worry, we understood at once THERE IS NO COMPETITION, only endlessly joyous varieties of experience.

WE BEGIN AND WE BEGIN AGAIN.
WE NOTICE HOW WE ARE MOVING THROUGH LIFE.
WE ARE LIFE.

The Story of Life ACT II

68

We Saw What Was Lost in the Name of Progress

In our fury to keep up with work, whether to prove ourselves to ourselves or to others, we wore ourselves out. Or, in our LOVE OF FUN AND PLAY, we sometimes forgot to rest and to restore. We shortchanged our gift of change through CREATIVE CONTRIBUTION when we failed to stop and replenish our bodies, minds, and spirits. Through the simple GIFT OF OUR PRESENCE in the day and through RESTFULNESS that led us to fully embrace the balance of work and play, we found our way FORWARD INTO FREEDOM and a life of blessing born of balance.

WE BEGIN AND WE BEGIN AGAIN.
WE BALANCE WORK, PLAY AND REST.
WE ARE LIFE.

69

We Stood Apart and Judged

We stood apart and judged the world as insufficient to meet our need. We asked, perpetually, if this was all there was, having cut ourselves off from ALL THAT WAS SEEKING US. In all our questioning, we were avoiding the current of our lives. With one foot in and one foot out, we STRADDLED TWO WORLDS and two ways of being. We could not truly know ourselves until we stood heart to heart and hand in hand, immersed in the plentiful WATERS OF LIFE that flowed to us and through us and, when we looked closer at the wonder, from us and because of us.

    WE BEGIN AND WE BEGIN AGAIN.
    WE STAND IN THE STREAM OF OUR LIFE.
    WE ARE LIFE.

70

We Fought the Flow

We made our own way, seeking to shield ourselves from the pain we associated with RELATIVITY OF RELATIONSHIP. Some of us thought it all an accident and learned to doubt what our souls longed to share. Others raised their voices to proclaim the truth, seeking converts or confession. Unbending, we fought against THE LIFE THAT WOULD SET US FREE until we found the grace to live our truth in grace and carry each other in so doing.

> WE BEGIN AND WE BEGIN AGAIN.
> **WE CARRY OUR TRUTH IN GRACE.**
> WE ARE LIFE.

71

We Stood on a Far Shore

There came a STILLNESS AFTER THE STORM. Sometimes, as we thought we were walking alone through our lives, we heard the distant melody and the sound of a rushing river deep within. We stood on the edge of our lives, met in the MOMENT OF CHOICE. There, we listened for the whispers of our soul and the still small voice that rang most true. We made our way back to the PLACES IN THE HEART we knew by heart as little children and felt ourselves finding our way home again.

> WE BEGIN AND WE BEGIN AGAIN.
> **WE LISTEN FOR THE SONG OF OUR SOUL.**
> WE ARE LIFE.

REVELATION • **Emancipation & the Restoration of Humanity**

This movement examines the landscape of **Who We Really Are** and how we are *Embracing a New Vision* for the nexus of change and a new humanity.

FINDING OUR WINGS • Dreams for a New World / Spirited Life • DAWN RICHERSON

The Story of Life
ACT III *The Sun Rises Full*

HUMANITY IS RAISED TO A HIGHER HARMONIC. A new life begins in promise and possibility. WE RISE TO GREET THE NEW DAY. So much changed. We have connected at last with **the fullest expression of who we are**, at home here in a world that is cradled in **an infinite grace**.

We come to **the work of transformation.** Ready for life's grand adventure, we step into the love we are, **knowing there is more**. The invitation is to a WHOLE NEW WAY OF FREEING OURSELVES. As you reconnect to **your unique and essential truth**, you help us collectively to create a new story of life and navigate the way ahead.

YOU ARE LOVE, a unique representation of the **One Love**. Together, we **assimilate this love** we are into our present reality and live from love. We live now into a new story, **embracing a new vision** for the nexus of change as we come to LIFE and live in full expression. We remember what it means to **be free spirits**. WE BEGIN AGAIN.

The Story of Life   ACT III

72

We Were Searching for the Answer

Scouring the distant horizon, looking down at our feet, we had searched high and low for the answer. We had awaited A REVELATION from the skies—some sign that now was the time. Uncomfortable with a swirl of questions and uncertainty, we hesitated, shielding ourselves from all we did not yet comprehend, missing THE KEYS TO LIFE WITHIN. As we brought compassion to music of the questions stirring in our hearts, we began to sway to the comfort of knowing there was more than just an answer YET TO BE REVEALED.

    WE BEGIN AND WE BEGIN AGAIN.
    WE MOVE TO THE MUSIC OF THE QUESTIONS.
    WE ARE LOVE.

The Story of Life　　　　　　　　　　　　　　　　　　　　　　　ACT III

73

We Were Cycling Through

Ever focused out there, we had fixed our attention on a tiny fractal of time, missing the MULTIDIMENSIONAL OPPORTUNITY found right here and now, within the portal we are. We had been waiting to find direction, forgetting it is we who are ourselves ETERNAL CYCLES OF CHANGE. Seeing we had been cycling round and round without connecting first within, we began anew with a new point of view and a fresh perspective, EVER EVOLVING in our knowing that we are fortunate agents of change in life's fertile fields of many growing things.

> WE BEGIN AND WE BEGIN AGAIN.
> **WE SEE OURSELVES AS A CYCLE OF CHANGE.**
> WE ARE LOVE.

74

We Seemed Strangers to Ourselves

We saw so much as lost and wasted and longed to save ourselves. We seemed strangers to ourselves. Leaving WONDER by the wayside, we busied ourselves responding to what seemed to matter most. Everything seemed an emergency. Desperately we searched for one another, forgetting again that the whole of our lives were a dance in A DREAM WE CHOSE. Meeting ourselves and one another again, we entered into beauty, returning to what mattered most. Valuing at last THE VALUE OF OUR LIVES we found meaning in art of getting to know ourselves. We began by exploring the territory of the soul and engaging in life refinement.

WE BEGIN AND WE BEGIN AGAIN.
WE ENGAGE IN VALUE REDEFINITION.
WE ARE LOVE.

The Story of Life ACT III

75

We Were in a Hurry or Stuck in the Waiting Game

We saw time stand still and understood it not. Still, we worried about running out of time. At the same time, we delayed our FULL EXPRESSION IN TIME. Waiting or in a hurry, we missed THE PROMISE WRAPPED UP IN OUR PRESENT. Eventually tiring of waiting in line, we slowed down one day. We looked around and saw time differently. ALL WAS SACRED. Time stood still and in the stillness we saw we were fully here and meant to fully share.

WE BEGIN AND WE BEGIN AGAIN.
WE STAND IN SACRED TIME.
WE ARE LOVE

76

We Held Our Breath

We held our breath, but nothing seemed to happen. Still accustomed to looking in every direction but within, we saw so much but missed entirely the point of the PARALLELS and REPEATING PATTERNS. It felt like meaningless repetition. We teetered on the verge of a radical discovery, awaiting a revelation that could only be revealed when we partook of it. On the deep inhale we found ourselves REVIVED AGAIN and saw all things coming back to life. The promise of protection held, hope in this light of a new day dawning for humanity had been more than just hopeful incantation. It had been LIFE'S FAITHFUL INVITATION to which we said yes again and again and again.

WE BEGIN AND WE BEGIN AGAIN.
WE BREATHE IN PROMISE REVEALED.
WE ARE LOVE.

The Story of Life — ACT III

77

We Veiled Ourselves in a Perpetual State of Delay

We had always looked out there, up to heaven and a home far, far away. Forgetting THIS GIFT WE GAVE OURSELVES, we were waiting for the gift of eternity that we thought could only come to us in the future. We are ever yearning to become free at last, unaware of the sheer veil that clouds the VISIONS OF GLORY we so diligently seek. In the unveiling and in the unfolding, we were met with the INTRICACY OF SIMPLICITY.

WE BEGIN AND WE BEGIN AGAIN.
WE SEE THE INTRICATE BEAUTY OF LIFE UNFOLDING.
WE ARE LOVE.

78

We Saw What Was Forfeited

Having long ignored what lay inside, we forgot that BEAUTY BEGINS WITHIN. Appalled at all that was going wrong in the world, we gave at first so little attention to our inner environment, forfeiting along with our responsibility for its condition the ABUNDANT GIFTS waiting there. When we surrendered without condition, we saw that life's love was without condition and that beauty was ever being BORN FROM WITHIN. This knowing we would never again leave behind.

>WE BEGIN AND WE BEGIN AGAIN.
>**WE KNOW THAT BEAUTY BEGINS WITHIN.**
>WE ARE LOVE.

79

We Pressed Hold

We compared ourselves to some imagined ideal, hiding from HUMBLE BEGINNINGS or a state of being we judged by the standards so long placed upon us by society. Much time had passed since we stopped to consider our HEART'S DESIRES. We denied ourselves, sometimes putting the life more abundant, here for us now, on hold until we felt we could look some imagined part. When we finally hit play again, we GOT BACK IN THE GROOVE of what feels good. Aligned with the fullness of our being in the fullness of time, we released the waiting game and FOLLOWED THE FLOW of love moment by moment, day by day.

WE BEGIN AND WE BEGIN AGAIN.
WE FIND WHAT FEELS GOOD.
WE ARE LOVE.

80

We Left So Many Dreams Behind

We saw now how we had left so many DREAMS FOR OUR LIFE behind and thought it all too late to begin again. We secretly wished for some other life or something more or other than what we had. On occasion we even wished to be other than where we were or were pretending still to be. Yet, we felt powerless to change any of it and so cast choice aside, forgetting it was OUR BIRTHRIGHT. When we finally decided there was no too late, we began again by choosing and choosing again.

WE BEGIN AND WE BEGIN AGAIN.
WE CHOOSE AND CHOOSE AGAIN.
WE ARE LOVE.

81

We Were in a Field of Fixed Circumference

We bound ourselves to a fixed circumference, keeping to what we saw as our designated FIELD OF EXPERIENCE. We lived lives defined by limitation, consumed by a litany of why we could not venture further into ALL THAT LAY UNEXPLORED in our lives and in our hearts. Being and becoming outside the bounds of limitation, though tentative at first, we found our way back to the free spirits we had always been. We explored, wandering with wonder, trying on the experiences to discover WHAT BRINGS OUT THE BEST in the best of us.

    WE BEGIN AND WE BEGIN AGAIN.
    WE FIND THE EXPERIENCE THAT BRINGS OUT OUR BEST.
    WE ARE LOVE.

82

We Lost Our Balance in Busyness

We busied ourselves with the business and busyness of life, thinking we must always be doing something, on the way to somewhere. We missed the DELIGHTS OF THE DAY. We failed to notice the wonder unfolding now, losing our balance as we favored forward momentum over stillness and the SAVORING THE MOMENT. We returned to center, cultivating the essence of life and in time finding ourselves again outside the matrix we had known, balanced now in a matrix of our SOUL'S TRUTH AND RADIANCE.

> WE BEGIN AND WE BEGIN AGAIN.
> **WE CULTIVATE PERSPECTIVE AND BALANCE.**
> WE ARE LOVE.

83

We Feared Changing Form

We feared death and even steered clear of LIFE'S DARING which required change. We felt reduced or somehow diminished by such an experience, and so deprived ourselves of the RICH EXPERIENCE life offered to us. All too often, we fixed ourselves to what seemed most safe and drew a circle for our lives based on this false centerpoint. Reconsidering, we saw at last the RELEVANCY OF CHANGE and considered how form relates to function.

> WE BEGIN AND WE BEGIN AGAIN.
> **WE CONSIDER FORM AND FUNCTION.**
> WE ARE LOVE.

The Story of Life ACT III

84

We Were Looking for Life in All the Wrong Places

Scouring the distant horizon, looking down at our feet, we have searched high and low for the answer. We waited for some REVELATION from the skies—some sign that now was our time. Uncomfortable with a swirl of questions and uncertainty, we hesitated, shielding ourselves from all we did not yet comprehend, and missing THE KEYS TO LIFE within. Unlocking the truth of how we were looking for life and love in all the wrong places, we chose a new way forward, embracing change as we sailed THE SOUL'S OPEN SEAS.

>WE BEGIN AND WE BEGIN AGAIN.
>**WE EMBRACE CHANGE.**
>WE ARE LOVE.

85

We Played a Game of Forfeiture

We forfeited so many opportunities, failing to take the CHANCE TO CHOOSE AGAIN. Overwhelmed by choice at times and feeling we had no choice in the moment that followed, we forgot that choice was merely an INVITATION TO CREATIVE CONTRIBUTION. We worried we would make a mistake from which there would be no recovery. We tied love and grace to condition and so reduced our own experience. But the game wasn't over. We only thought it was. SURPRISED BY SECOND CHANCES, we joined life's celebration and made a creative contribution.

WE BEGIN AND WE BEGIN AGAIN.
WE CELEBRATE CHOICE AND CREATIVE CONTRIBUTION.
WE ARE LOVE.

The Story of Life   ACT III

86

We Were Stalling

Wavering, we wondered if we had only imagined this NEW FREEDOM THAT WAS OURS. We listened again to others who told us we were merely dreaming and so shortchanged THE WILDNESS AND THE WONDER in our reduction of a truth that was essential. Coaxed back into an alluring, half-wakened state, we stalled so near the finish line which was to be OUR BEGINNING AGAIN. Seeing this truth two minutes before the end, we got back up and set our eyes on prize of presence, only to discover that it too was A PASSAGE TO BEGIN AGAIN to know more of who we truly are.

>WE BEGIN AND WE BEGIN AGAIN.
>**WE HOLD FAST TO THE TRUTH OF WHO WE ARE.**
>WE ARE LOVE.

87

We Were Afraid to Trust Again

Afraid again to TRUST OURSELVES AND THIS LIFE, which was far more expansive than once we had imagined, we climbed back into the box. Bound so long by tradition, culture, and religion, we feared what we might discover in realms within and beyond—those we now sensed we were FREE TO EXPLORE. We forgot we were created free and beyond the bounds of fear. Somehow we found the courage to fly again, this time INTO BLUE SKY and back to love again.

WE BEGIN AND WE BEGIN AGAIN.
WE UNBIND OURSELVES AND FLY FREE.
WE ARE LOVE.

The Story of Life ACT III

88

We Debated Daring

We wished to be as the great explorers. Ready now for LIFE'S GRAND ADVENTURE, we stood dazed and confused, puzzled by life's unfamiliar shores. We searched for a golden compass, forgetting that OUR SOULS WOULD ALWAYS LEAD US HOME. We debated whether to make life's journey full. Seeing how all our pondering was merely pretense, we came clean to the current and DARED TO RIDE THE RAPIDS.

WE BEGIN AND WE BEGIN AGAIN.
WE RISK LIFE'S JOURNEY.
WE ARE LOVE.

89

We Were Perplexed

We tamed our own spirits, buckling beneath the weight of all those people and systems who told us it was time to get serious about this life. We noticed when we were overlooked that these acts of DARING COURAGE AND HONOR seemed invisible to those for whom we had risked our very lives. We saw PROVISIONS that seemed meager and the humble way of our life and wondered what to do. Seeing we were overthinking it all, we chose the pirate's carefree spirit upon the daring seas and reclaimed the SPIRIT OF PLAY the child in us had left behind. No longer lost, no more perplexed, we simply took life in a day at a time.

WE BEGIN AND WE BEGIN AGAIN.
WE RETAIN OUR SENSE OF PLAY AND ADVENTURE.
WE ARE LOVE.

The Story of Life ACT III

90

We Feared the End

In ourselves or another, we faced the hardest choice of all. GOODBYES had always seemed the end. We thought goodbye was forever. We thought our lives to be but a fleeting opportunity and merely temporary. And so it was we delayed our VOYAGE OF DISCOVERY, fearing its eventual end and not realizing we are ever beginning again. Upon this RETURN TO RADIANCE and our long-awaited remembrance of the love we are, we greeted the day WITH REVERENCE and found joy in the beginning that came at what we thought to be the end.

    WE BEGIN AND WE BEGIN AGAIN.
    WE KNOW THE END IS THE BEGINNING AGAIN.
    WE ARE LOVE.

For a Whole New You
For a Whole New Way Forward

Cultivating Essence from the Matrix of Soul is now available in hardcover, paperback, and e-book editions. Order this 13th anniversary edition of the book online at DawnRicherson.com and Soul-Simple.com and at bookstores and retail locations around the world. Contact the author to inquire about bulk discounts.

Rooted in the magical and the miraculous, we are growing back toward the ground of being, moving into a new era, rich in love. The opening words of this new collection of the *Cultivating Essence* core passages invite us into a whole new way forward together that begins when you embrace a whole new you. We begin within.

Each succinct and seemingly straightforward "seed for life" is surprisingly layered, each soul-activating text like a love letter that awakens you to wholeness and the roots you in the magical and the miraculous found when you reconnect to your soul. The lifeseeds inside the book are pathways to purpose that form a map to come back to life.

This book takes you through three movements of change to awaken the world within, find your forward flow, and embrace a new vision for the nexus of change in your life. It is "a manual for the many" that lays out a direct and daring map for whole life thriving as you remember the light, the life, and the love you are at your core.

More Books by This Author

Cultivating Essence from the Matrix of Soul
Awakening the World Within
Finding Our Forward Flow
Embracing a New Vision
Seeds for Life

All Systems Go
Birds of a Feather
True Identity
A Reconciliation of Light
12 Doors of Abundance
Energetic Perspectives

Journey to the Heartland
Journey to Sacred Wholeness
Sacred Partnership

Many Rivers Flow
Across the Seas of Time
Testament: A Half-Life in Poems
The Magda Poems

From the Heart of a Child
To Sin by Silence

www.ingramcontent.com/pod-product-compliance
Lightning Source LLC
Chambersburg PA
CBHW040001080526
44586CB00027B/2839